First World War
and Army of Occupation
War Diary
France, Belgium and Germany

16 DIVISION
48 Infantry Brigade,
Brigade Trench Mortar Battery
31 October 1915 - 1 January 1916

WO95/1975/9

The Naval & Military Press Ltd
www.nmarchive.com
Published in association with The National Archives

Published by

The Naval & Military Press Ltd

Unit 10 Ridgewood Industrial Park,

Uckfield, East Sussex,

TN22 5QE England

Tel: +44 (0) 1825 749494

www.naval-military-press.com

www.nmarchive.com

This diary has been reprinted in facsimile from the original. Any imperfections are inevitably reproduced and the quality may fall short of modern type and cartographic standards.

© **Crown Copyright**
Images reproduced by permission of The National Archives, London, England, 2015.

Contents

Document type	Place/Title	Date From	Date To
Heading	1975/9 Brigade Trench Mortar Battery 31 Oct 15 Jan 16		
Heading	16 Div 48 Bde 48 Trench Mortar Bty. 1915 Oct To 1915 Dec		
War Diary	1/20,000 Sheet 78 N.W. B.79 a 33	31/10/1915	14/11/1915
War Diary	In the Field D.19.21	14/11/1915	01/01/1916

1975/9

Brigade Trench Mortar Battery.

31 Oct 15 — Jan '16

~~Army Troops~~

16 DIV 48 Bde

48

TRENCH MORTAR BTY.

1915 OCT to 1915 DEC

(1687)

Army Form C. 2118

WAR DIARY
or
INTELLIGENCE SUMMARY 118th Brench Mortar Battery

(Erase heading not required.)

Instructions regarding War Diaries and Intelligence Summaries are contained in F. S. Regs., Part II. and the Staff Manual respectively. Title Pages will be prepared in manuscript.

Place	Date	Hour	Summary of Events and Information	Remarks and references to Appendices
Po.000	3/10/15		Very wet. Kept in tch. drains	
	1/11/15		Interfere between trenches [illeg]. between the dug outs.	
Hat 98	2/11/15		Quiet. Commenced with fund. to act M.L. new dug out collected.	
N.W.	3/11/15		Removed pond for pits amm. stn. drained water dug out.	
M99 a 33	4/11/15		Cleared trenches. drains [illeg].	
	5/11/15		do	
	6/11/15		Dried one round dud.	
	7/11/15		No cycloe. [illeg] 7 days in only.	(a 11/15

R.A.M. Roberts
Major. 118th T.M.B.

1875 Wt. W593/826 1,000,000 4/15 J.B.C. & A. A.D.S.S./Forms/C. 2118.

Army Form C. 2118

WAR DIARY
or
INTELLIGENCE SUMMARY 48th Trench Mortar Batty
(Erase heading not required.)

Instructions regarding War Diaries and Intelligence Summaries are contained in F. S. Regs., Part II. and the Staff Manual respectively. Title Pages will be prepared in manuscript.

Place	Date	Hour	Summary of Events and Information	Remarks and references to Appendices
Sheet 28. NW B.29 a.33	8/9/15		Fired 6 Rds (of duds) All landed in enemy trenches.	
	9/9/15		Drained emplacement slightly. Renewed dug outs.	
	10/9/15		Removed left 1½" for 6.S.19 as emplacement got unbearable.	
	11/9/15		Target drain not for emplacement	
	12/9/15	10 am	at	
	13/9/15	10 am	Removed tools & dried dug outs.	
	14/9/15		Renewed dug outs again as hut had fallen in overnight.	
	15/9/15		Ye man took ill the week and stop in hay the high emplacement free from water as for trench above in renewing dug outs trenches.	

R.A.M.N. Croste
in g__ of Trench 48" TM B

Army Form C. 2118

WAR DIARY
or
INTELLIGENCE SUMMARY
(Erase heading not required.)

48th Trench Mortar Battery

Place	Date	Hour	Summary of Events and Information	Remarks and references to Appendices
In the field O.19.21.	14th	14.30	Position of unit sheet 20.nw Sheet 28 N.W. B.28 central.	
	15th	15.30	Removing gun from 18.72 to old water-cuttings	
		16.45	Reconstructing, filling cans for gun position 18.19.	
		17.30	Short bomb stood and drawing water	
		18.30	Finning gun position & strengthening hutts	
		19.30	Fixing alternative gun position & drawing & ammunition & strengthening hutts	
		20.30	Strengthening hutts, lifting gun beds.	

R.C. Upton Lt. R.G.A.
Comdg. 48th Trench Mortar Battery

Battery rest billet
B.19.b.8.5.

48 Trench Mortar Battery Army Form C. 2118

WAR DIARY
or
INTELLIGENCE SUMMARY
(Erase heading not required.)

Place	Date	Hour	Summary of Events and Information	Remarks and references to Appendices
In the field	21/5		Billet. Building & strengthening dug-out for men. Trenches. Fired four 3¼ bombs in retaliation to Rifle grenades.	
	22/5		Quiet in trenches, endeavouring to drain position of guns, mens dug-out in Pillbox, strengthening walls of billet.	
	23/5		Drawing gun position in trenches. Strengthening billet & at rest camp.	
	24/5		Shifting mens billets to above map location. Quiet in trenches.	
	25/5		Erecting tents & squaring up mens camp, digging latrines &c	
	26/5		Drawing positions of trench, erecting cookhouses for men.	
	27/5		Cleaning up of billets.	

R Colquhoun
2/Lt R.G.A.
Cmdg 48 Trench Mortar Battery
48th Divn

Army Form C. 2118.

WAR DIARY
or
INTELLIGENCE SUMMARY.
(Erase heading not required.)

48th Trench Mortar Battery.

Place	Date	Hour	Summary of Events and Information	Remarks and references to Appendices
In the Field	29/5		Belly Lyres Sheet 28 N.W. B.19.8 & 6.	
	29/5		Removing prop of collapsed dug out, bringing back spare beds from trenches.	
	1/5		Taking up new ammn. boxes (4) to trenches, cleaning ammn. & putting in boxes	
	30/5		Reconstructing collapsed dug-out, shifting camp	
	1/5		Siding tents, continue 2 latrines in new billet, cleaning gun position & rebuilding parapet.	
	2/5		Cleaning up of camp, rebuilding trench dug-out.	
	3/5		Cleaning beds brought from trenches, checking stores & improving camp.	
	4/5		Cleaning camp, cleaning & putting out mini dug-out in trenches	

R. Appleson /Lt. R.S.A.
Comdg. 48th Trench Mortar Battery.

C. Coles Capt.
49 (W.R.) Div. T.M. Bats

Army Form C. 2118.

WAR DIARY
or
INTELLIGENCE SUMMARY.

48th Trench Mortar Battery.

(Erase heading not required.)

Instructions regarding War Diaries and Intelligence Summaries are contained in F.S. Regs., Part II. and the Staff Manual respectively. Title pages will be prepared in manuscript.

Place	Date	Hour	Summary of Events and Information	Remarks and references to Appendices
In the Field	6/5		Rest Billet. 20,000 Sheet 28. NW B.19.a.8.5	
	7/5		Draining gun emplacement, rebuilding trench dug-out, selecting site for Canal Bank dug-out	
	8/5		do — do — cleaning ammn. commenced new main dug-out	
	9/5		do — do — building dug-out on Canal Bank.	
	10/5		removing roof of collapsed bomb store, cleaning ammn. — do —	
	11/5		rebuilding bomb store, oiling ammn, & drying charges. — do —	
	12/5		cutting down from gun position & bomb store strengthening dug-out. — do —	
	13/5		strengthening & draining bomb store & dug-out. — do —	

R Colquhoun Lt RGA
13/5. Comdg 48th Trench Mortar Battery.

Army Form C. 2118.

WAR DIARY
or
INTELLIGENCE SUMMARY.
(Erase heading not required.)

4 8th Trench Mortar Battery

Place	Date	Hour	Summary of Events and Information	Remarks and references to Appendices
In the field	12/5		Built 20,000 sheet 28 NW. E.19.6.8.5. 15" Gun Position 19.19. H/P gun can be carried across dugouts	
	13/5		Completed dugout on canal bank.	
	14/5		Cutting stairs round dugout on canal bank.	
	14/5		Asking out & drawing gun emplacement	
	15/5		Drawing ammn.	
	16/5		Drawing & erecting huts	
	17/5		Erecting huts & clearing up gun emplacement	
	18/5		Refinishing parapet & drawing hurd	

R Claydon 1/Lt RGA
Cmdg 28th Trench Mortar Bty

Army Form C. 2118.

48th Trench Mortar Battery 1/31/16

WAR DIARY
or
INTELLIGENCE SUMMARY.

(Erase heading not required.)

Instructions regarding War Diaries and Intelligence Summaries are contained in F. S. Regs., Part II. and the Staff Manual respectively. Title pages will be prepared in manuscript.

Place	Date	Hour	Summary of Events and Information	Remarks and references to Appendices
In the field	19/1		Billet 2000 Sheet NW B.19.b.8.5	
			Draining & baling out dug out, trenchs & canal bank, double detachment	
	20/1		N guns on canal bank. removing gun from forward position	
	21/1		removing ammunition stores from forward gun	
	22/1		removing ammunition stores from forward gun	
	23/1		cleaning up guns & ammunition in store	
	24/1		selecting forward dug out for new gun, carrying up gun & ammunition	
	25/1			

R Ingraham Lt RHA
Comdg #8 Trench Mortar Battery

48th Trench Mortar Bty

Army Form C. 2118.

WAR DIARY
or
INTELLIGENCE SUMMARY.
(Erase heading not required.)

Place	Date	Hour	Summary of Events and Information	Remarks and references to Appendices
Sue Sus	26/5		Billets 2000 Shut 27 NW B.10d.9.9.	
	27/5		Changed billets	
	28/5		Stores & Guns brought down from Canal Bank and sent to Poelem with the exception of two guns near Dawson City	
			Stores & Guns checked and cleaned	
	29/5		Kit Inspection	
	30/5		Stores & Guns brought down from Canal Bank to new Gun Belts	
	31/5		Two Gun and Stores handed over to 4th Divisional Trench Mortar Bty at 6.30pm	
	1/6		Moved into Rest Billets. Old Billets cleaned up	

W. G. Kinkhoney
Lt
Condg. 48 Trench Mortar Bty

1/6/16

Condg. 48 Trench Mortar Bty

www.ingramcontent.com/pod-product-compliance
Lightning Source LLC
Chambersburg PA
CBHW081512160426
43193CB00014B/2666